THE BOOK OF GENESIS: G.O.A.T TALK

WORDS to MOTIVATE, MANIFEST, & MOVE

Genesis Renji

Copyright © 2021 Genesis Renji

All rights reserved

No part of this book may be reproduced, or stored in a retrieval system, or transmitted in any form or by any means, electronic, mechanical, photocopying, recording, or otherwise, without express written permission of the publisher.

Cover design by: Genesis Renji
Printed in the United States of America

To Richon, thank you for inspiring me to do this.

To you, thank you for reading this, I hope these words move you to be the GOAT I know you are.

To me, you the GOAT.

CONTENTS

Title Page	1
Copyright	2
Dedication	3
Preface	9
Foreword	11
PART I: MOTIVATION	13
DIVINE TIMING	15
THE LITTLE THINGS	17
EXCELLENCE	19
SETTLING	21
YOU'RE CLOSER	23
DIESEL	24
FLOWERS	26
LOVE YOURS	27
ENJOY THIS LIFE	29
TAX 'EM	31
GROWING	33

KEEP WHAT FITS	34
BE ACCOUNTABLE	35
MOVE AROUND	36
F.T.J	37
BET ON YOU	38
THE GOLDEN RULE	40
PART II: MANIFESTATION	41
RECOGNITION	42
BELIEVE IT	44
IT'S YOURS	46
LIVE YOUR DREAM	48
GRATITUDE	49
PART III: MOVEMENT	51
DON'T WASTE TIME	52
KEEP WORKING	53
CONSISTENCY	55
APPLY PRESSURE	56
CHOOSE VIOLENCE	58
DROP IT	60
ACCEPTANCE	61
LETTING GO	62
D.O.	63
RUN IT BACK	64
C.R.E.A.M	65

SAVE FOR THE SUN	66
REST	67
SWITCH IT UP	69
THE MANTRA	71
About The Author	73

PREFACE

It is important to preface this how I preface all "advice" I give. *ahem*:

I DON'T KNOW SHIT. These are personal thoughts and opinions from my life experiences. Proceed.

The Book of Genesis is inspired by an online interaction I had with my friend Richon Martená. After commenting on a Facebook status Richon posted, she responds by saying "I'm finna start a second book of Genesis for your quotes lol".

This triggered me to complete an idea I already had, gather my tweets and Facebook statuses and bundle them into one place for people to digest them for future reference and motivation (or laughter, your pick).

The hardest thing to do is stay inspired, motivated, "in-mode", in the zone. More times than not we need positive triggers that kickstart us into gear. By the time we get into that flow-state or that zone, we forget what got us into it. So it's hard to return back to that point of inspiration or encouragement in our times of need.

This book. This talk. This is that anchor point. Most of

these quotes are things I've said on a whim to Facebook or Twitter, or they were responses I've given to friends and acquaintances in the moment.

The intuitive response is typically the right one, and it's also the scariest. So the point of this is for me to say to you the things you need to hear but may not know or may be too afraid to say out loud.

But don't fucking worry. Because I will. Buckle up bitches.

◆ ◆ ◆

FOREWORD

by Richon Martená

When I first met Gen, years ago, I remember being in awe of his star power. The way he stood on his artistry and was unapologetic about who he was, was captivating.

I knew I wanted to be a part of Gen's community but I didn't expect it to start by him linking me with his barber, after mine flaked. This was our first time meeting in person and this man ribbed my shoes lol. It was the perfect icebreaker and ever since he's been consistently coming through when I need advice or some GOAT talk.

I'm extremely proud of Genesis for starting and finishing this project. It's easy for us to table things we begin but I told him, "You gotta nut Gen, what's the point of sex."

He's given me and others alike countless gems. It was only right that he put this book together so that people who may not be a part of his community benefit from them too.

Here's to finishing strong.

- RICHON MARTENÁ

PART I: MOTIVATION

words to inspire

DIVINE TIMING

There is no right time.

I am a fan of planning and patience. I don't always like practicing patience, but I love the power and results that come from it.

However, I don't use patience as a crutch. I don't wait for the "right time", because the right time doesn't exist.

There's your time and there's Time. And your time will always lose to Time when you're playing the waiting game.

Act on the things you want. Adapt to whatever the results may be. But stalling, procrastinating and using the excuse "I'm waiting for the right time" is the biggest crock of shit I've ever heard. It's a poisonous mentality and one you don't need.

There is no right time, there is only right now.

◆ ◆ ◆

THE LITTLE THINGS

You can't build a beach without sand. The little things matter most.

Dreams are the most important anchors. Ironically. The shit that we think about and envision is what keeps us most grounded and working towards something so that our existence isn't a waste.

Many dreams are robust and attractive, as they should be. But we can get so caught up in making those big things come to fruition that we only focus on performing big actions.

But what's the quickest way up a mountain? A step at a time. Steps. Not strides. The little things are what matter most. The pyramids weren't dropped in Egypt premade. They were meticulously and intentionally built. Brick. By fucking brick.

From the shore the beach doesn't seem like much. Just

a vast stretch of free forming earth that gets slapped with water when the moon says so.

But when you sit down and really take a look you realize the earth that is holding you up and bending it's will under your weight, is really a collection of billions of smaller grains of sand that collectively make one grander vision and purpose. You can't build a beach without sand. The little things matter the most.

◆ ◆ ◆

EXCELLENCE

Excel on all fronts at all costs.

I'm an "army brat". I come from two veteran parents and being in a military household there's an almost unspoken law: don't half ass shit.

Whenever my brothers and I would get in trouble, our mom would discipline us with military workout routines. If we did a lazy jumping jack, we had to keep going. If our butts were too high in the air for push ups, we had to keep going. That carried over into regular life tasks for me.

Everything I do I have to do thoroughly and completely. So I make sure I only do shit I care about, because the things I don't give a fuck about will be half assed and we can't have that.

"Well, why can't I do it halfway, nobody will notice."

Your name and your work will enter many rooms far sooner than you will. Don't let your first impression be one of someone who doesn't commit and deliver when they are expected to.

Growing up, my older cousin Joe would teach us martial arts in the backyard and he would always say, "How you spar is how you will fight".

Commit to the practice. Be diligent in the little things. Don't half ass anything. You're only cheating yourself.

◆ ◆ ◆

SETTLING

You can get impatient in the building phase but don't sacrifice the integrity of what you're working towards for a brief moment of satisfaction. Don't. Fucking. Settle.

The human brain is wired to release dopamine (aka "The Reward Chemical") when things are achieved in order to give you a sense of accomplishment, excitement, and joy.

The brain is also trained to recognize the patterns that fulfill this feeling. This is great for routines, workouts, knocking out immediate goals and building momentum.

The problem comes when you're working on something and it begins to take longer than anticipated. Or it becomes more difficult than you planned. Now you're experiencing frustration, impatience, anxiety, and anticipation. All because you KNOW what's at the end of the long, gruesome road you've been religiously traveling and dedicated to.

And in those moments, that's when you'll look for any small win or feeling that even slightly resembles achievement and accomplishments. And that's where you fall into the trap of SETTLING.

Whatever you do. Settling is not the option. That momentary lapse of judgement where you sacrifice your quality and integrity to feel "better" (because you don't feel good, you just feel better than you did for that moment), you'll come out of that feeling and realize you wasted time and energy instead of continuously committing to that vision and dream you had. You compromised. Don't.

◆ ◆ ◆

YOU'RE CLOSER

Whatever you're doing, don't let up, you're almost there.

It's easy to get discouraged about the things you're chasing. You can feel like "This shit ain't coming fast enough".

I've been there, I'm still there, but you have to remember you're almost there. Each day you're up and going after the shit you want is a day you're closer to reaching whatever it is you're aiming for.

Keep going, it's right there.

◆ ◆ ◆

DIESEL

Talk yo shit.

Aye man. Say man. Let these fuckers know you that muhfucka. You're not to be overlooked or played with.

Remind them you the fucking goat. Tell these broads you the baddest bitch. Let them losers know you're a superstar, the top of your class, the lead salesman at your job. Brag on yourself.

Who will praise you if you don't? No one would've called Muhammad Ali the greatest if he didn't tell MFs he was the greatest. They were still trying to recognize him as some black boy from Kentucky who just became a boxer. No. That man was the fucking GOAT. And why?!

BECAUSE HE SAID SO.

SAY SO.

◆ ◆ ◆

FLOWERS

Give yourself your flowers.

Humans have this infatuation with showing love and appreciation to people when they can no longer receive it.

Don't wait on people to give you the love and appreciation and credit you deserve.

Appreciate your damn self. Gas you up. Give yourself the props and kudos you deserve.

Who can love you better than you? Not a fucking soul. Start praising yourself more. You deserve it.

◆ ◆ ◆

LOVE YOURS

Make sure yo people know you love em. Even if y'all ain't where you used to be, make sure they know.

Life is short. Literally, it's only 4 letters. Even death is longer than life.

Don't waste life not telling people how you feel about them while you can. Especially if you love them.

I have a cousin who means the world to me. A big brother, a best friend, a confidant, an idol. He's not dead, but due to health complications, he's not the same as when we were kids. And I often wonder if I told him how much he really meant to me while he was able to completely comprehend and truly appreciate it.

There are days when the people we love may frustrate us and we don't want to deal with them, but even when my brothers and I are arguing or at odds with each other, we remind one another: "Aye, I don't like you right now" or "You sound stupid as fuck... but I love you".

Let the people you love know that you love them because those days are not promised for long.

◆ ◆ ◆

ENJOY THIS LIFE

This life is too short to complain and too long to waste.

This thought came to mind while I was thinking about death. Sad as shit, I know. But a very immediate reality.

Any of us can be gone at any time and we wouldn't be able to do anything to stop it.

Sit with that.

Now ask yourself, "How am I treating life?"

This life is to be experienced. Enjoyed. Taken advantage of. Shared. Complaining doesn't stop it from moving forward. Wasting a one time experience is just fucking stupid.

Enjoy this shit. Don't complain about anything. ANYTHING. It's pointless. Change it or remove it. That's literally all you can do.

Don't waste this gift that's been given to you. Everyday somebody doesn't see the same sunrise you do. Be thankful you got to see it and live knowing you're not taking it for granted.

◆ ◆ ◆

TAX 'EM

Every task comes with a ticket.

I don't do shit for free. Not a fucking thing. My time and my actions will be compensated.

Now. Aht aht aht. Don't get to tweeting "pay me to talk to me", sit yo $5 ass down. Compensation isn't always financial.

You can do a favor for someone knowing that favor will be paid back in kind and at a higher value than what you've offered.

You could do work for someone free of financial charge but with the knowledge and guarantee that the person you're helping will leverage their power and influence to help you when the time comes.

You can also just tax these muhfuckas for whatever you

believe you're worth, and can get paid that much.

Every task comes with a ticket. Every action is followed (and even sometimes preceded) with an invoice.

Pay the fucking fee.

◆ ◆ ◆

GROWING

In the midst of people having you fucked up you learn your limits and where to grow.

Boundaries are uncomfortable. Confrontation is uncomfortable. It is human nature to avoid the things that make us uncomfortable, they're unpleasant and feel threatening to our existence.

But when you encounter that discomfort, you learn exactly what you can put up with, what you absolutely won't put up with, and you begin to grow as a person in strength, fortitude and bravery.

◆ ◆ ◆

KEEP WHAT FITS

I tried modesty, it doesn't fit me.

I'm that muhfucka. Won't even beat around the bush. I am the fucking greatest thing existing. And that's how I personally feel (and I got stats to back it). So why in the fuck would I smother my greatness and energy that I exude to make another muhfucka comfortable?

Ain't me. Can't be. Won't be.

If there is a "quality" or a label that people are trying to place on you and attach to you that doesn't fit who you are don't let them. Snatch that shit off and never let them put it back on you.

We only rock tailor-made compliments over here.

◆ ◆ ◆

BE ACCOUNTABLE

We don't complain about what we prayed about. Keep it pushing.

Don't ever fix your lips to bitch about the same shit you wished for. Show grace and dignity in every moment you're fortunate enough to experience the things you asked for.

You wanted it. You take all accountability for what comes with that. The good. The bad. The ugly.

You asked for it. It's yours. Own it.

◆ ◆ ◆

MOVE AROUND

You'd accomplish more if you stop getting in your own way.

As much as we can be our biggest supporters, we can also be our biggest obstacles.

Procrastination. Self-sabotage. Doubt. Fear. Pride. All of that shit. Don't be the reason you don't get shit done.

◆ ◆ ◆

F.T.J

Fuck that job.

I cannot stress this enough: FUCK. THAT. JOB.

If you aren't being treated well, if you aren't being properly compensated, if you aren't being respected, if you aren't being appreciated: FUCK. THAT. JOB.

These people will replace you in a heartbeat. Their business doesn't stop because you leave and your livelihood shouldn't be at risk because their only priority is making the quarterly profit target.

As Andrew Henderson said, "Go where you are treated best".

There is more and there is better.

◆ ◆ ◆

BET ON YOU

Fuck a job, you don't need it.

This is ONLY for the entrepreneurial spirits. If you are somebody who needs security and peace of mind in order to live, please, skip this quote.

Now… if you're still reading this. You don't need that job. Specifically my creatives.

The last job I worked I almost hurt myself doing it. It was at a mattress removal and installation company and we were working on a rainy day… shitty weather for a shitty job.

So, I'm on the truck, I'm taking down the automatic, sleep number bed frame (this is a large, heavy ass box of metal and mini engines). As I'm stepping backwards to lay the box down, I slip because the truck floor is wet.

Somehow I was able to throw the bed frame box away from me as I fell, and luckily (by the grace of God almighty) we left the old bed on the floor of the truck.

As I landed on that old mattress, I had to lay there and just pause. My work partner asked was I okay and I told him, "Yea... just... gimme a moment."

All I could think about was my dad cursing me the fuck out for getting hurt working a job when I shoulda been in the damn studio.

Fuck. A. Job. You don't need it. You have a passion. You have something you care about that you can devote your life to and make a living. A very good living.

It won't be easy. It'll be harder than anything else you've ever done before. But I promise you, the freedom you have, the peace of mind you attain knowing you're only doing YOUR SHIT on YOUR TIME and getting paid YOUR RATES... it's worth every feeling and emotion.

◆ ◆ ◆

THE GOLDEN RULE

Bet not be trash.

I run a label, the House of Renji. An indie label that hosts an eclectic array of talent. Whenever one of my artists, Emmitt James, sends me his music to release I respond the same way:

"Bet not be trash"

Whatever you want to do, that shit better not be trash. Deliver excellence in every action you take. Save that watered down bullshit for the practice squad, we professionals over here.

◆ ◆ ◆

PART II: MANIFESTATION

words to repeat

RECOGNITION

How do you want to be recognized as something or someone you don't see yourself as? I don't go a day without calling myself the GOAT. Don't go a day without recognizing who you are.

If you follow me or know me you know people refer to me as the GOAT ('Greatest Of All Time' for you juvenile seniles that may not know).

"Well, why do they call you the GOAT, Gen?"

Because, boys and girls, that's who I carry myself as. That's who I address myself as. That is who I am. And because they see it and recognize it, they respect it, acknowledge it and ,in turn, spread it.

You can't expect people to treat you how you want to be treated when you don't treat yourself that way on your own.

I don't go a damn day without reminding myself I am the fucking GOAT. The best shit since sliced bread and silverware. I literally have moments in the day where I pause whatever is going on, look to the person closest to me and tell them, "Fam. I'm really that muthafucka."

And you know what they do? You Ghaddamn right. AGREE. Because they see it. And they not only see it, they BELIEVE IT. Because I believe it.

You will never be the doctor, teacher, parent, nurse, pilot, writer, bad bitch, playboy, sweetheart, good son, loving daughter, girl genius, or billionaire that you want to be until you start to be. When you want to be something, you begin to MOVE like that. TALK like that. BREATHE like that. Your entire existence is dedicated to embodying the being you want to become.

Because you see it. You fucking feel it and now you need the rest of the universe to feel it too.

Make a declaration of who you are. And make that declaration daily in everything you say, do, and think. I bet people start to see you and treat you the way you've been wanting.

◆ ◆ ◆

BELIEVE IT

A big part of being ready is believing you can do it.

I was on the phone with my business partner Chloé and we were talking about next steps, goals, etc. A major point in the discussion for us was when would we know we were ready for the next level in our lives? That next step we were aiming to take but didn't know if we had all the pieces for it.

I told Chloé, "A big part of being ready is believing you can do it".

You have to carry yourself in the manner you want to express yourself. You have to move the way you want to live. You have to embody the life you envision.

Now, I'm not telling you to drape Birkins from your shoulders and buy SRT Hellcats with a $10,000 down payment and 34% APR. Don't start doing dumb shit.

Be intentional about how you live. If you want to be 10 pounds lighter and slimmer, buy clothes that'll motivate you to change your dietary habits and workout to fit into them. If you want to travel around the world, start in your own country, hell your own city. So many people from my hometown don't go to the other side of the city, not knowing there's an entire world waiting to be shared and discovered if you're open to it.

Figure out what you want to do. Who you want to become. Then, a day at a time, take small steps towards bringing that desire(s) into reality.

The life you want is available, you just have to start living it.

❖ ❖ ❖

IT'S YOURS

Everything is mine already. It is all by design already.

There has to be a sense of delusion in your life to achieve the things you want. You have to believe beyond a shadow of a doubt, against all odds and statistics that the things you want to achieve are LI-TER-ALL-Y made for you and only you to achieve.

"Now why is that, Gen?" Because, reader, when an objective is met with focused actions, it is inevitable. When you think of a red car, what's the first fucking car you see?

So when you consistently drill this mentality into yourself that "everything I want is already mine" you are in turn projecting to the universe all that is yours. And the universe will deliver all that is yours upon you.*

Footnote: all manifestation requires A C T I O N. The Bible says faith without works is dead. Put the walk behind the talk, too.

◆ ◆ ◆

LIVE YOUR DREAM

Walking like I got it so it ain't foreign when I get it.

Live in your truth. That's what they be saying right?

Exist how you imagine. I have a song called "02-911" where I rap about how I used to drive my 2002 Ford Taurus like it was a Porsche 911, because that was the luxury I wanted. So I had to live like I had it.

I drove that Ford with the same confidence and prestige (and mostly speed) as I would've driven that Porsche.

Live as if you already have it. When it comes to you (and it will) you'll already know what to do with it and it won't feel strange. You've already been there, it just caught up to you.

◆ ◆ ◆

GRATITUDE

Regardless of the positions I'm in, I'm forever grateful to be able to pursue the things I want in life.

Chances are if you're reading this you're not where you would like to be in life. Hell, I know I'm not. And that's okay.

There's a reason you are where you are right now. Maybe you still have something to learn. Maybe you still have someone to reach. Maybe yo ass just ain't doing what the hell you know you need to do. It happens. And that's okay.

Acknowledge where you are in life and appreciate it. Because I guarantee you, before this, there was a time where you didn't like where you were at and didn't think you'd get to where you are today. It seemed impossible. But you made it happen.

I start everyday the same way. I wake up, grab my

phone, go to Twitter and tweet "Thank you for today #TMC".

Gratitude is the first step to prosperity. Give thanks.

◆ ◆ ◆

PART III: MOVEMENT

words to perform

DON'T WASTE TIME

Do what you can while you can.

This quote initially came as an ego thing. I have to remind people I'm really the one and they need to take advantage of whatever leniency I feel like I may be granting.

Now, all of that aside, don't waste time.

You only have right now. Take advantage of RIGHT NOW. Not tomorrow. Not an hour from now. RIGHT. NOW.

The fuck you still reading for, go do that shit.

◆ ◆ ◆

KEEP WORKING

Everybody wanna work when they see it's working for you.

You know what people love the most: results. They love to feel like they've done, won or attained something. It's an addictive feeling.

Do you know what people love more than results? Not having to work for them.

Be honest, the easy way is the most attractive and most sought after. I am the king of "fuck that shit". I don't do it unless I want to. But I also know some things have to be done in order for me to continue doing what I want.

I've been in situations with artists and producers who don't want to do the work I request of them because it's "too much" or it's an "extra step" or they just don't wanna fucking work.

UNTIL…. they see my work is paying off. Now they're

doubling back and trying to work. Nah fool, it's too late.

If you're working and nobody else is, get away from them. That attitude and that energy will only slow you up and frustrate the hell out of you.

This quote in particular is to reassure you that people will come back around when they see your success.

They will peek into the windows of the house you built and knock on the doors of opportunity you once presented. Leave their asses on the porch. Keep building your legacy.

◆ ◆ ◆

CONSISTENCY

Stay consistent.

Consistency is like snowflakes, there are no two ways that look the same.

But to be consistent doesn't mean executing at a fast, never ending pace. No, it means to execute and perform time after time at the same rate that you expect of yourself and at the quality that is expected of you.

Don't relax, don't get lazy, don't slack. Stay consistent in everything you do. It's the only way to separate yourself and win.

◆ ◆ ◆

APPLY PRESSURE

Stand on these niggas necks.

My big sister Brittney has been telling me to stand on these niggas necks for the better half of a decade. And I've been living it religiously.

"Stand on these niggas necks" means to apply pressure, consistently and constantly. Don't ever let up. Be an unforgettable force to be reckoned with.

There will be periods where you feel like you gotta ease up on the competition because you got a lead or you're "killing it".

Fuck that.

Stay on top of it. You never know what the other person has in the tuck. You never know who's watching you. Don't give them a window of opportunity. Never let up.

THE BOOK OF GENESIS: G.O.A.T TALK

❖ ❖ ❖

CHOOSE VIOLENCE

Richon: They heard you the first time.

Gen: That's why we choose violence the second time.

The most frustrating part of being a person, an adult for that matter, is having to repeat yourself TO OTHER ADULTS.

You heard me the first time. You're as grown as I am, correct? So why the hell do I have to repeat myself?

I personally believe that the older we get the more violence is justified (not necessarily physical violence; but abrupt, direct responses and actions). Because, come on, at this point in our lives we just fucking know better. At this point everything we do literally comes down to one word: principle.

So if you're fucking off the principle of the matter, I should be able to receive my interest in blood.

There will be people who pretend they don't hear you

when you speak, especially when you speak politely and respectfully. Some people only respond to outrage, disrespect, and chaos. Understandable, some people are crazy like that, but make that the last resort. Always start with restraint and respect, because you can always say you gave them that option.

But never overextend yourself trying to make nice with a person who only responds to war. You get one chance, anything after that, bets off.

◆ ◆ ◆

DROP IT

We tend to drag ourselves through this psychological torture chamber of "what ifs", "whens" and "maybes". It's really hard to just accept the present sometimes.

Aye fam. Whatever happened, happened. Let that shit go.

The "I would've done this". Pointless.

"I could've done this". Dead that shit.

"I wish this". If wishes were bitches I'd be a pimp.

Drop. That. Shit. It happened. Either appreciate it or forget it. Move on. Live for today, for right fucking now. Because one day you'll be wishing you had lived in the moment you're overlooking right now.

❖ ❖ ❖

ACCEPTANCE

Accept it as is.

There's too much shit in this life we have absolutely no control over, and yet somehow we make those things the main focus and bane of our entire existence.

Put the energy you do have into the things you can actually do something about. Let the rest of that shit be.

Remember the serenity prayer:

> God, grant me the serenity to accept the things I cannot change; courage to change the things I can; and wisdom to know the difference.

❖ ❖ ❖

LETTING GO

Let that shit go.

Read it. Do it.

◆ ◆ ◆

D.O.

Drop out.

If you've been thinking about it, this is your sign to do it.

It can be school, work, a project, a relationship, a friendship that no longer serves you. Drop out of it.

Committing yourself to things you are not passionate about is a one-way ticket to depression and failure. You're not a failure and you don't want to be depressed.

Drop out. The worst thing that happens: you realize it was a mistake, or you see you just needed a break and that thing is still there.

Bounce.

❖ ❖ ❖

RUN IT BACK

Fuck that job.

Just to reiterate and stress the importance of this point. Take care of YOU.

◆ ◆ ◆

C.R.E.A.M

See the bag. Get the bag.

Chase the money, chase the money. There is always an opportunity to profit in any situation. If you see it, take it.

Don't hesitate to make a play for yourself to win. There's a million ways to get rich, you need at least seven.

◆ ◆ ◆

SAVE FOR THE SUN

Save that money for them sunny days, too.

We were all brought up to "keep some cash in the shoebox" and "have a piggy bank" or a "rainy day fund". To save for emergencies.

That's important, critical, and necessary. But save for the sunny days, too. Put cash aside to enjoy days doing things you love with the people you love.

Money is a tool to be used, use that tool to enjoy the finer things in life. Scared money don't make money and scared money don't make memories.

❖ ❖ ❖

REST

Enjoy the down time; work never dies.

Coming from me it seems almost hypocritical, but, I can speak from experience: the work doesn't leave.

It's always there. There is always something that needs to be done, an errand that has to be run, a box that needs to be marked 'completed', a list of things to-do.

You will never do it all. I'll say it again for you stubborn fucks and Virgos who may be reading this: you will N E V E R do it all. Don't kill yourself trying to do an impossible task.

Rest. Relax. Reflect. Reset. Even God rested. If an omnipotent, omnipresent, omniscient entity took a breather, then your barely got out of bed at 8 A.M. ass can too.

Sleep. Eat. Sit. Be still at times. Why work yourself to death when you can't bring anything with you? Take advantage of the life you were given.

Enjoy the fruits of your labor. Give yourself some fucking credit. You did a great job. You are still doing a great job.

The work will always be there. But you won't always be here. Savor every moment. Those may be the only things you bring to the other side.

◆ ◆ ◆

SWITCH IT UP

Pivot.

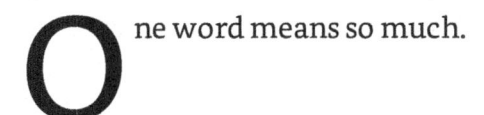

One word means so much.

A pivot, by definition, is a verb which means to turn. In basketball the pivot is used to maintain control when you've stopped dribbling and still move around to get a better view of the floor before making a pass or shot.

Pivot in this instance is used in a similar way. To gather and to turn.

Situations (will arise *Usher voice*) happen in life that force us to halt in our tracks. And most people, when halted, stay stuck. Which is the last fucking thing you want to do. Stopping slows down momentum, loss of momentum is a loss of energy. losing energy is losing power. Now you're powerless and stuck.

Instead of being a deer in headlights when life does it's "life-shit", you should pivot. Maintain control but shift your perspective. Find or create a new opportunity for you to progress.

The most recent example can be the COVID-19 pandemic. It halted the entire world, and it forced a lot of people to pivot. Folks who no longer had jobs created new hustles for themselves to stay afloat and have been doing okay with them.

Don't be afraid of making a small change in direction, you'll see a whole new landscape. It could be better for you, too.

◆ ◆ ◆

THE MANTRA

Know self. Love self. Trust self.

I have this tattooed on my arm. This is one of my many personal mantras.

Know who you are. Self awareness is the greatest superpower on earth. When you know who you are no one can tell you who you are and have power over you.

Love whoever it is you discover you are. When you are at peace with who you are you will be at peace with the world around you and willl know how to move within that world without compromising your identity.

Trust yourself. Your intuition is never wrong. Ever. Don't ignore it.

The constant factor in this mantra is 'self'.

Put yourself first. Rely on yourself first. The rest will

fall in line.

♦ ♦ ♦

ABOUT THE AUTHOR

Genesis Renji

Genesis Renji is the GOAT.

Follow @genesisrenji on all social media platforms.

www.genesisrenji.com

Made in the USA
Coppell, TX
01 January 2024